Lightning Bolt Books™

Horse Sports

Lisa Idzikowski

Lerner Publications ◆ Minneapolis

For my family

Lerner Publications Company
An imprint of Lerner Publishing Group, Inc.
241 First Avenue North
Minneapolis, MN 55401 USA

For reading levels and more information, look up this title at www.lernerbooks.com.

Main body text set in Billy Infant Regular. Typeface provided by SparkType.

Lerner team: Sue Marquis

Library of Congress Cataloging-in-Publication Data

Names: Idzikowski, Lisa, author.
Title: Horse sports / Lisa Idzikowski.
Description: Minneapolis, MN : Lerner Publications, [2025] | Series: Lightning Bolt Books: horse lover's library | Includes bibliographical references and index. | Audience: Ages 8-11 | Audience: Grades 4-6 | Summary: "From speeding around tracks to playing games, horses compete in a lot of sports. Discover horses running around barrels, making soaring jumps, and much more. Young readers learn about how horses and riders work together"—Provided by publisher.
Identifiers: LCCN 2023037488 (print) | LCCN 2023037489 (ebook) | ISBN 9798765626061 (library binding) | ISBN 9798765628904 (paperback) | ISBN 9798765634929 (epub)
Subjects: LCSH: Horse sports—Juvenile literature. | Horsemanship—Juvenile literature. | Kentucky Derby—Juvenile literature.
Classification: LCC SF294.23 .I38 2025 (print) | LCC SF294.23 (ebook) | DDC 798—dc23/eng/20231020

LC record available at https://lccn.loc.gov/2023037488
LC ebook record available at https://lccn.loc.gov/2023037489

Manufactured in the United States of America
1-1009871-51940-10/6/2023

Table of Contents

Sporty Horses

Horses line up at the starting gate. Nervous jockeys grab their reins. When the bell rings, the horses rocket down the track.

In horse sports, horses run, jump, pull carts, dance, and more. Riders are important because they train, steer, and guide the horses.

The rider guides the horse as it jumps.

Horses and riders have to trust each other to work together.

Horses and their riders also play games or practice special moves much like ballet. In horse sports, riders and their horses work together as a team.

What Moves!

Dressage is a sport where horses move to music. They move like dancers.

Riders guide them as they step, walk, and skip about. Riders and horses practice and learn to move their feet and bodies correctly.

A horse shows its skills.

The horse and rider compete together. Judges watch each team and give them points. The team with the most points wins.

Each rider and horse is a team.

A horse slides in a reining event.

In reining, horses perform routines. They do spins, slides, and circles.

Vaulting focuses on the riders. As the horse trots or walks in large circles, the rider or riders do jumps, kicks, and flips on top of the horse.

Riders perform difficult moves in vaulting.

On the Trail, Track, or Course

In some sports, horses and riders jump over objects, race other horses, or pull carriages. In cross-country, horses run long distances. They soar over logs and hills.

In jumping sports, horses leap over tall objects. In an arena, a horse jumps over fences.

A horse leaps over a hurdle.

Horses pull wagons in carriage driving. Each team races toward the end of the course.

Horses race around the track pulling carriages.

In races, horses gallop on a track. Jockeys steer their animals toward the finish line.

Horses gallop around barrels or poles in rodeo races. The fastest horse that doesn't knock over or miss an obstacle wins.

A horse turns around a barrel.

Let's Play Games

Games played on horseback are exciting. Horseball is like basketball played on horseback. Teams score by shooting the ball into a hoop.

A polo match is about one to two hours long.

In polo, players from two teams of four players ride horses. Players swing mallets to hit a ball between goalposts to earn points. The team with the most goals wins.

Horses and their riders work together to compete in sports and win.

Horse Sports and You

Horses and their riders can compete in many different sports. What sport would you like to compete in with a horse?

Fun Facts

- In reining, horses sometimes look as though they are skating across the floor due to how smooth their movements are.
- Safety first if you ride a horse! Wear gear such as a helmet and sturdy riding boots.
- The Kentucky Derby, held annually since 1875, is the longest-running horse race event in the United States.

Glossary

dressage: a competition in which horses perform special movements in response to signals from their riders

jockey: someone who rides horses in races

obstacle: something that blocks a path

polo: a game played by two teams of four players who ride horses while using long mallets to hit a wooden ball into a goal

reining: a horseback sport in rodeos where riders guide their horses through a pattern of circles, spins, and stops

rodeo: an event where people compete at riding horses and bulls, catching animals with ropes, and other activities

routine: a series of movements that are part of a performance

steer: to control the direction in which something moves

vaulting: an athletic sport performed on top of a horse

Learn More

Britannica Kids: Horseback Riding
https://kids.britannica.com/students/article/horseback-riding/633449

Gitlin, Marty. *Ticket to the Triple Crown.* Ann Arbor, MI: Cherry Lake, 2023.

Herweck Rice, Dona. *Horse Play.* Huntington Beach, CA: Teacher Created Materials, 2023.

Kiddle: Equestrianism Facts for Kids
https://kids.kiddle.co/Equestrianism

Kiddle: Kentucky Derby Facts for Kids
https://kids.kiddle.co/Kentucky_Derby

Krenn, Cara. *Horseback Riding.* Minneapolis: Lerner Publications, 2025.

Index

Photo Acknowledgments

Image credits: Greg Pease/Getty Images, p. 4; John P Kelly/Getty Images, p. 5; Lucio Dias Filho/Getty Images, p. 6; Somogyvari/Getty Images, p. 7; Merbe/Getty Images, p. 8; Tim Platt/Getty Images, p. 9; PROMA1/Shutterstock, p. 10; Ventura/Shutterstock, p. 11; Stefan Holm/Shutterstock, p. 12; Zocha_K/Getty Images, pp. 13, 20; Pieter Sorber WorldRC/Shutterstock, p. 14; Romilly Lockyer/Getty Images, p. 15; LifeJourneys/Getty Images, p. 16; sunsinger/Shutterstock, pp. 17, 20; Glowimages/Getty Images, p. 18; Uwe Krejci/Getty Images, p. 19.

Cover: Zave Smith/Getty Images.